50 Frequently Asked Questions by Fish Farmers with Detailed Answers

50 Frequently Asked Questions by Fish Farmers with Detailed Answers

Anthony Adefarakan

AQUATON KONSULTS

CONTENTS

INTRODUCTION

50 FREQUENTLY ASKED QUESTIONS WITH ANSWERS

ABOUT THE AUTHOR

A NOTE FROM EL-ADONAI: THE CHAIRMAN OF AQUATON KONSULTS

Beloved Reader,

You are highly favored and enviably blessed to have a copy of this manual in your hands at this moment, because all you will read therein are products of My inspiration.

As far back as Genesis 1:20-22, on the fifth day of My creation work, I commanded the waters to bring forth fishes of every kind, and they all came to being at My command.

And because they came at My command, all their activities – feeding, breathing, swimming, reproduction, growth etc – are regulated by Me. As their Creator, I determine which one survives or not, which one grows well or not among other outcomes of their existence (Ps. 115:3).

I am so interested in fishes, and I demonstrated this in the ministry of My Son – Jesus Christ – when He was with you on earth. For instance;

1. In Matt. 4:18-22, the first disciples I chose for Him were fishermen (fish dealers).
2. In John 6:5-13, He fed the 5,000 with five loaves of bread and two fishes.
3. In Matt 15:32-38, He fed the 4,000 with seven loaves of bread and few little fishes.
4. In Matt 17:24-27, I sent Him money through a fish to pay His tax.

5. In John 21:5-6, He gave His disciples abundant harvest of fishes.
6. In John 21:9-13, He cooked fish for His disciples to eat.
7. In Matt. 4:19, He termed soul winning as "fishing for men's souls".
8. In Luke 5:1-11, He filled Peter's net with fishes until his boat began to sink.

It therefore implies that for you to succeed in this your fisheries project, you really need the help of My Son - **Jesus Christ** – who knows so much about fishes. I will recommend you accept His Lordship over your life and the project so that He can show you the way to succeed. Remember, "Without Him, you can do nothing" (John 15:5). Tell Him these if you want Him to help you: *"Dear Lord Jesus, I give my life to you as my Lord and Savior so that you will help me. Lord Jesus, I dedicate my spirit, soul, body and this fisheries project to you; help me and guide me. Thank you for saving me. Now, my success is guaranteed in Jesus' Name. Amen".*

Congratulations! Now go ahead, read the manual and apply the principles written therein, your success is guaranteed. All the best!

With love from:
El-Adonai,
Chairman, Aquaton Konsults

INTRODUCTION

Aquaculture, popularly referred to as fish farming is a fast growing business around the world, attracting many investors from diverse sectors. Clarias happens to be the most cultured species in the tropics and it has been proven to yield good returns at market size.

However, many of these investors dabble into the venture with little or no information at their disposal. Some just attended a day "sensitization" seminar/workshop and thereafter kicked off as fish farmers; while some just saw their neighbours, friends etc practicing it, and having land and space as well jumped into the business. As a result of this uninformed venture into an unknown business, many of such farmers have recorded a great deal of loss in one way or the other over time.

On the other hand, the seemingly successful ones are also devoid of certain information capable of improving their practice – raising certain questions on their minds.

It is therefore in order to correct the wrong foundations laid by the untrained farmers as well as to reinforce those of the trained ones that we put together this material capable of totally transforming the entire venture of fish farming if correctly applied.

The questions contained in this handbook are those encountered during our training sessions, consultancy services etc and many of them are potential questions in many farmers' mind. That is why we have taken good time to explain them; and the correct application of the information gathered from this piece will definitely improve your practice.

50 FREQUENTLY ASKED QUESTIONS WITH ANSWERS

1. How can I know good and healthy fingerlings or juveniles at the point of purchase?

Answer:
There are ways to know. But I quickly want to point out to you that fish seeds are not to be procured just anywhere, the credibility and integrity of the farm should be ascertained before going into a transaction with them. To the question now, the fish you are to procure must be agile-swimming properly, (not just lying at the base). It must be responsive to feeding – a feeding fish is a healthy fish. Also, there shouldn't be signs of infection on the fish – the skin must be neat and fresh, the tail intact and the head not with any white patches. With these checks in place, you can go ahead and procure them.

2. As a starter, should I stock fingerlings or juveniles?

Answer:
It all depends on you – your level of knowledge about the management practices involved. But as a starter, we always recommend stocking juveniles. A fingerling is a fish of about 4 – 5 weeks old while juveniles are about 8 – 10 weeks old. The disadvantage of you stocking fingerlings is that they are too tender for you to handle. Also, at this stage, the shooters (jumpers) are still emerging and their removal may lead to you stressing the whole population. In addition to these, weather variation and

water parameter fluctuation can lead to mortality because their immunity is low at this stage and they have low tolerance. But as juveniles, they are more stable, capable of withstanding the stress of transportation, handling, etc. Even in water parameter fluctuations or disease conditions, they are more tolerant. It's advisable to stock juveniles as a starter, then as you master the practice, you may start stocking fingerlings.

3. How do I know the number of fish my pond or tank can contain?

Answer:

There is what we call stocking density, which is a function of the species being cultured, their sizes and the dimension of the culture medium. In catfish culture, the stocking density is about 40 – 60 fish/cubic metre for concrete and mobile tanks while for earthen ponds, it is about 60 – 80 fish/cubic metre. These densities can be adjusted and manipulated depending on the farmers' ability to manage and handle the stocks. In recirculatory system, the stocking density is always higher, sometimes up to 200 – 300 fish/cubic metre being an intensive culture system.

Now, to calculate the number of fishes your pond can contain; follow these steps:

- Take the measurement of your pond and get the dimension in metres i.e length, breadth and depth.
- Multiply the measurement and your dimension will be in m^3 (cubic metre).
- Then, multiply the answer by the number of fishes required to be stocked per cubic metres
- The answer is the number of fishes to be stocked and produced in that pond e.g. in a concrete tank of 8m x 5m x 1.5m = $60m^3$. $60m^3$ x 40 fish = 2400. That is, 2400 fishes will be stocked in that pond. If it is in earthen pond; it can be up to $60m^3$ x 80 fishes = 4800 fish. That is, 4800 fish will be stocked in the earthen pond of the same dimension.

4. What is the standard pond size?

Answer:
There is no hard and fast rule about pond size. It all depends on the farmers' choice, available space and his management ability. But this must be put into consideration, fishes require good space for growth, so the pond should not be too small or tight. It is when there is enough space for the fishes to swim and play around that their growth is enhanced; through adequate feed consumption and effective metabolism. This makes them come for more feed; and the more they eat, the better they grow. However, there's a FAO (Food and Agriculture Organization) recommendation for the depth of the pond; it is said not to be more than 2.0m so as to avoid oxygen depletion at the pond bottom. In any case, your pond size is standard if it can successfully produce your target stock size.

5. How many times am I expected to feed my fish daily?

Answer:
Clarias is a species of catfish that eats voraciously; nonetheless, feeding regimes can still be established for them. These regimes depend on the farmer. You can make it 3 hours interval or 4 hours interval that is, 9am, 12 noon, 3pm, 6pm or 8am, 12noon, 4pm, 8pm or as it suits you. Just ensure you feed adequately at each regime and don't over feed in a regime since there are still other regimes. If you do this consistently, the fish will be disciplined enough to adjust their feeding to your time. Try this out and you will see what I'm saying.

6. How do I know the times to change the grades of my fish feed?

Answer:
Catfish feed on various grades of feed depending on their age and of course their mouth size – that is, what their mouth can take when feeding. And in practice, it's most likely that you will have to feed a higher grade after feeding a particular grade for about 2 – 3 weeks. This is because a 2nd or 3rd week fish is not the same as that of 1 week. For instance,

Dizengoff feed comes in these grades: 0.1 – 0.3mm, 0.3 – 0.5mm, 0.5 – 0.8mm, 0.8 – 1.2mm, 1.2 – 1.5mm, 1.8mm, 2mm, 3mm, 4.5mm, 6mm, and 10mm. The first five (5) grades are collectively referred to as starters, for use in fish hatchery and nursery. A 4-day old fish can feed on 0.1-0.3mm, and after two weeks, they commence 0.3 – 0.5mm when their mouths would have been able to pick the feeds. This continues at 2 weeks interval until the fishes become juveniles (8-10 weeks old) when they can switch to 1.8mm, 2mm and so on until they become adults capable of taking 6mm and the finisher (10mm). To know when to change your feed grade, you will notice your fishes outgrowing a certain grade. When this is discovered, don't introduce the new grade sharply as they may not respond to it. Instead, starve them for half a day and then introduce it or feed the former one in the morning regime and skip the regimes in between until the last one when you will introduce it. This is also applicable when you are changing their feed, say from foreign (floating) feed to local (sinking) pellet. They will adapt. However, if there are wide variations in the sizes of your fish population, sort them first, so as to know what grade you are to give. This is because some may not be able to pick what others are able to pick, which can cause poor or ineffective feeding.

7. What quantity of feed should my fish take on a daily basis?

Answer:

There are two ways to this. First is the discretional feed to satiation method while the second is feeding according to body weight. Catfish converts the quantity of feed given to flesh (in weight). That is, for a catfish to reach 1kg in weight, it must have consumed nothing less than that same kilogram of feed (when the feed conversion ratio is 1:1). The first method is what is commonly employed by uninformed farmers who just feed without putting cost and judicious feed utilization into consideration. The fact that your fishes are rushing at your feed does not necessarily imply they are feeding. Infact, most times, in the process of rushing, they push a great percentage of the feed down and they end up as waste – this can be discovered when draining their water. Clarias have short intestines, and they don't feed for long before they are full, only that they will soon be hungry again due to quick digestion and absorption. And that is the reason for establishing feeding regimes, so that the initially fed feed would have undergone digestion and absorption before feeding another one. If you keep feeding when they are done with feeding, you are simply wasting your feed.

On the other hand, sampling before feeding is a way of ensuring feeding in the right proportion and consequently cost effectiveness. As earlier said, catfish feed by body weight and their feeding rates differ at various body weights.

This chart represents the feeding rates at various fish sizes

S/N	Size of Fish	Feeding Rate
1.	5g – 10g	5.5 - 6%
2.	10g – 50g	4.5 – 5.5%
3.	50g – 100g	4.0 - 4.5%
4.	100g – 250g	3.0 – 4.0%
5.	250g – 500g	2.0 – 3.0%
6.	500g – 750g	1.5 – 2.0%
7.	750g – 1kg	1.1 – 1.5%
8.	1kg – 1.2kg	0.9 – 1.1%
9.	1.2kg – 1.5kg	0.8 – 1.0%
10.	1.5kg – 2kg	0.7 – 0.9%

For example, if the daily feed of a population of 1,000 juveniles is to be determined, half of the population (500 pcs) can be taken out and weighed together. If they weigh 5,000g, it then suggests that the average body weight is 10g (got by dividing the total weight by the number of fishes sampled i.e. 5,000g ÷ 500 juveniles).

Then, multiplying the average body weight which is 10g by the 1,000 juveniles in the pond, we have 10,000g as the total weight of fish in that pond.

If you check where 10g average body weight falls on the chart, it is 5.5 – 6% feeding rate.

Using 5.5% we have;

5.5/100 x 10,000 g (total weight)

= 550 g

This means, that population of 1,000 juveniles will feed on 550g of feed (whatever the grade) on a daily basis. This however will not be fed at once, but it will be divided into the daily regimes. This exercise is to be repeated at 2 weeks interval so that the fishes, which must have grown more, would not be underfed. You will as well be able to check the performance of the feed on your fish as you take their weight difference (within 2 weeks). In addition to feeding the fishes well, you can calculate the amount you are spending or to spend on a particular population. Your results at each sampling must be documented for monitoring. For more information on this, you can pick a copy of our training manual on catfish farming.

8. When is the best time to change my water?

Answer:

There is no hard and fast rule on water changing in catfish farming. However, there are certain factors to consider before changing the water. For instance, if there is algae bloom i.e. when the pond water changes to thick green colour due to algae production, leading to turbidity which is lack of transparency, the water can be changed. Also, if the water is giving off an offensive odour like that of rotten egg (Hydrogen sulphide (H_2s) odour); it simply means the level of waste in the water is high, mostly from uneaten feed; and to prevent ammonia build up, the water has to be changed and if possible, the tank cleaned. Aside these, you may also change your water if the alkaline level is too high or whenever you see the fishes hanging on the water surface. This can however be partial or total, depending on the reason(s) for changing it. But take note, you are not to feed when you are about changing their water as it can lead to much stress and mortality.

9. What are the things to do for my fish to grow well?

Answer:
Two principal things. Feed them adequately with highly nutritious feed (having all the necessary ingredients for growth represented) and give them enough space to grow i.e stock appropriately. Catfish grow by converting the feed fed to flesh, and it's the flesh that results in weight. Thus, the better and adequate the feeds given, the better and bigger the fish will grow. On the other hand, when there's space, the fish metabolize easily – they digest their food and come for more. In addition to these two principal things, you must ensure a good culture environment in terms of conducive water parameters, disease free medium and highly hygienic practice. Note this however, if you get stunted fish and stock those, all the above mentioned points will not work. Watch your fish source.

10. What parameters do I need to take note of in ensuring good water for the fish?

Answer:
This is a very good question. There are certain parameters that make catfish thrive in any given water body. They are:

- **pH:** This is the amount of hydrogen ion concentration in the water i.e. the degree of acidity or alkalinity in a given water body. And it ranges from 1 -14 having 7 as the neutral point i.e. 1 – 6 is acidic, 7 is neutral, while 8 – 14 is alkaline. Thus, for proper catfish culture, the optimum (conducive) pH is between 6.5 and 8.0. Once you check your water, using a pH meter, it should give you a value within this range, that's how you can be sure you're culturing your fish in a conducive water medium.
- **Temperature:** This is referred to as the degree of hotness or coldness of a body. Catfish, being tropical fish thrives best at a

temperature of 27°c – 30°C. A thermometer can be used to get this.
- Turbidity and transparency: 0.30 – 0.60 m
- Dissolved oxygen:5.00 – 8.00 mg/l
- Carbon(iv)oxide:1.00 – 5.00 mg/l
- Ammonia:0.01 – 0.05mg/l
- Ammonium:30 – 60 mg/l
- Nitrite (NO_3):< 50 mg/l
- Nitrate (NO_2):0.01 – 0.03 mg/l

To check for all these, a water parameter test kit can be procured from any Aquaculture related store.

11. When do I sort my fish and how?

Answer:

Sorting is an exercise that should take place at 2 – 3 weeks interval. The sorting done at the earlier stage of the culture is often to prevent cannibalism, when shooters are separated from the rest of the population. Failure to do this may result in the bigger one's preying on the not very big ones, thereby reducing the population. The second type of sorting however, continues even to maturity and the essence is to ensure uniformly sized populations, preventing stiff competition for feed and space i.e. having the right number and sizes of fish stocked in the ponds. Then, to the how? It's simply by looking out for the shooters and removing them – that's the first type. But for the second type, you will have to drain the water completely, bring the population out (if they are not many), sort by hand and return to the prepared ponds (tanks). If they are many, you can demarcate the tank (pond) with say a plank or something related and do the sorting right in there. Take note of this please, no feeding should be done before sorting, and it's either done very early in the morning before the sun comes up or in the evening when the sun must have gone down. You put fresh water after the sorting and allow them to rest for about 1 hour before commencing feeding.

12. What ways can I employ to ensure effective aeration in my tank/pond?

Answer:

Aeration, which can otherwise be called oxygenation is the process of making dissolved oxygen available in the water. And this can be achieved through the use of electric aerators, turbulence, agitation etc. These aerators when in use generate bubbles in the water, thus, making dissolved oxygen available. And in the case of agitation, you can lay a perforated pipe across your tank and as it showers on the water, it splashes and makes dissolved oxygen available. Also, you may run flow through and with that, you make dissolved oxygen continuously available. That is, regulating the inflow and outflow simultaneously.

13. What feed is the best for catfish as there are many of them?

Answer:

This is true. There are many feeds in the market. But the best feed is the one that enables your fish to meet your production target. That is, if you want to produce your fish to reach market size in four months, the feed that assists you to achieve this is the best feed for your fish. To help you further, there are certain nutrient requirements that must be met if a particular species of fish must do well. For instance, for Clarias spp, the fingerlings require feeds with 35 – 40 crude protein, 12.0% lipid, 0.5% phosphorus, 1.0% calcium, 0.005% Vitamin C, 1.0% micro vitamins, 1.0% micro minerals etc to perform well (NIFFR/ FAO). For juveniles, it is 30 – 40% CP, 12.0% lipids etc. Thus, to know which the best feed is, check the nutritional label to find out what makes up the feed. Once you discover the composition can meet the nutrient requirements of your fish, go ahead and get it. Your fish will appreciate your effort by eating it well and converting it to the needed flesh. However, watch out for expired and mouldy feeds, they are capable of generating nutritional diseases in your stock. Feed only fresh feeds.

14. I am incurring too much cost in feeding my fish, how do I check this?

Answer:
It is very easy to fall into the temptation of overfeeding these fishes, which ultimately leads to lots of uneaten feed and the consequent ammonia build up in the water system. To reduce your cost of feeding, you'll have to find out what your fish need and give them just that, not more. You can sample some of them so as to get their average body weight, which will determine their feeding rate. You can check the answer to question number 7 for details. You don't feed emotionally, you feed with knowledge and understanding.

There's also another method, although not popular. Catfish and Tilapia can be reared together in what is called polyculture system. Tilapia is known for its highly prolific propagation. They become sexually mature in 3-4 months and once the two sexes are present, reproduction takes place, yielding so many offspring. These offsprings however serve as good food to the catfish, and by so doing, they are not only feeding but also controlling the population of the Tilapia, making the water a conducive ecosystem. From practice, it is discovered that catfish reared under such condition depend less on external feeding and they still do well. You can try it and experience what I'm saying.

15. I discovered the barbels (whiskers) of my fish are becoming whitish, what do I do?

Answer:
This is one of the symptoms of infection; and the moment you discover it you drain the water to a reasonably low level – say 20 – 30% water level from the pond bottom. Then treat with any of these: Aquaceryl plus, Keproceryl WSP, Fish biotics, Potassium permanganate ($KMnO_4$) and salt. You leave the treated water for about a day or two and record you're observations. If they appear better, raise the water to the normal level and continue managing them. But if any of them is badly affected, remove it and treat it in isolation. When it's well, you return it. Minimize feeding during treatment.

16. I stocked 5,000 pcs of fingerlings, and 6 weeks later I brought them out, only to find 4,000pcs, what could be responsible?

Answer:
In answering your question, I will like to draw your attention to the fact that the fingerling might have been wrongly counted at the point of stocking i.e. may be they were not up to 5,000 pcs. But if you really ascertained they were 5,000 pcs and in 6 weeks, you could only get 4,000 pcs, without noticing any serious mortality during the period or anyone coming to harvest some, then the only possibility is cannibalism. By this, I mean they must have eaten themselves.

Please note this, if you stocked them in an earthen pond, an additional possibility is the fact that some unharvested fish in the pond (unknown to you) might have consumed them. Whenever fish in earthen ponds are harvested, some escape by hiding themselves in the mud, and the moment you put water, they come out. If you stock fingerlings under such condition, predation is bound to occur. But in concrete tanks, it can only be due to cannibalism. Cannibalism occurs due to size differences – i.e. a condition whereby a bigger fish preys on the smaller ones, even if they are of the same age. To correct this however, sort your fish population regularly until they become averagely uniform in size and stock at the right stocking density. Six weeks is too long a period to leave fingerlings without sorting. So many shooters would have emerged, capable of trimming down the population. Refer to the explanation in question number 11 for more details on sorting.

17. Predatory birds are troubling my fingerlings, how do I control them?

Answer:
This is simply by covering your tank, you can get a carpenter or welder to construct a frame for you. The frame is to be netted with chicken mesh reinforced with mosquito mesh nets. This will not only prevent the birds, it'll also prevent other flying ants that may be disturbing the fish.

18. My fish's skin is looking pale – as if the skins are white, and I'm afraid they may die, what do I do?

Answer:
What you have just described is one of the symptoms of nutritional disease caused by dietary deficiencies. It is an anaemic condition caused by the deficiency of folic acid. In this case you have to check the feed you're giving to them. But if your feed is good and they still look pale, although active; then change your water completely and give them a short salt bath i.e treat them with salt for a short period before raising the water to the normal level. They'll be fine.

19. My water is always turning green no matter how I change it, what can I do reduce or even stop this?

Answer:
Greenness of water actually depicts productivity i.e. a good and productive water by reason of the presence of phytoplanktons in it. These phytoplanktons e.g. green algae are plant microorganisms which photosynthesize and multiply as sun makes contact with the water where they are. This is what leads to the green colour of the water. This is fine in the earthen ponds as there will be zooplanktons to control their populations. But in concrete tanks, what we always have is algae bloom (i.e. total and thick greenness of the water) with no zooplankton naturally occurring to feed on them. This is where the problem comes in. To correct this once and for all; shield or cover your pond. You can do this by building a structure over the tanks using roofing sheets. Without your pond water being exposed to sunlight, there'll not be any algae bloom on them. Or on the other hand, you keep washing your tank each time you notice it.

20. Is Clarias the only species of fish that I can culture? What other species can be cultured?

Answer:
There are many other species of fish that can be cultured. They include *Heterotis niloticus, Lates niloticus, Tilapia zilli, Oreochromis niloticus, Channa obscura, Heterobranchus bidorsalis, Heterobranchus longifilis,* etc. They are culturable species, only that you'll have to understand their physiology, habitat requirement, feeding pattern, reproductive behaviour among other facts to culture them successfully. For instance, Tilapia Spp is a pelagic fish (surface dweller) and it is herbivorous i.e plant eater, thus, you won't be successful by raising Tilapia on zooplanktons (animal microorganisms) because they are not carnivorous.

To culture any species of fish, get information on how it is being cultured from the right quarters – research institutes, farms already culturing it or through the internet. They have varying culture practices.

21. I have a hatchery, and anytime I hatch, the hatchlings die in 2 – 3 days, this has been recurrent, what do I do?

Answer:
Hatchlings are very delicate to handle and as a result, adequate preventive measures must be taken to ensure their survival. Therapeutic care at this stage is hardly effective.

To your question, the main thing to suspect is your water. There are certain pH and temperature ranges that can sustain catfish hatchlings. It's most likely your water is acidic i.e. it has a low pH. The ideal pH range for the fish is between 6.5 and 8.0 while the temperature range is 27^0C – 30^0C. At incubation, it must be ensured these ranges are in place, and if not they can be boosted by soda ash or bicarbonate of soda just to elevate the pH and they can be covered to elevate and maintain the normal temperature. With these in place, they'll survive.

22. How do I know good broodstocks?

Answer;
There are things to check. Firstly, the age of the fish. A good broodstock must be at least 12 – 15 months old – i.e. a mature broodstock. Next to this is the weight, no broodstock should be less than 500g. In fact, a

mature fish should have outweighed that. Then for the males, the genital papillae must be elongated and tough; not short and tender – although the final test is at slaughter. But for the females, you must be able to notice a soft rounded belly indicating a gravid fish. Also, the genital opening will be round with a reddish colour. These are external features capable of guiding one in selecting good broodstocks. For the males however, no male is good until dissection; if it has milky (cream like) milt, it is good but if it is watery, it is not good, no matter what features must have led to its selection.

Lastly, the history of the place of purchase can also guide in forecasting their production ability. Have the ones purchased from the farm been productive before? If yes, you can try them. . But I will like to say here that it is not very safe to buy males and females from the same source so as not to encounter in breeding which will lead to weak and poorly immuned offsprings. But with parents from different sources, the risk is minimized.

23. *Where can I sell my fingerlings and table size fishes?*

Answer:

You can sell them anywhere there's demand. For instance, to sell your fingerlings, you must be able to identify those into grow out farming i.e. those who don't engage in fish breeding, but only purchase and stock. If you are consistent, they'll remain your customers for as long as they are practising. Beyond this, you can put up handbills, posters etc just to create awareness, and before you know it, you'll be contacted. As for the table size, the market is very wide – you can create relationships with restaurants, hotels, pepper soup joints, market women, party organizers, co-farmers who may have demand beyond their supply capacity, neighbours, etc. you can as well engage print media advertisement. The challenge here however is that you must always be having supply to meet the demand so as not to lose the customers. If you are not satisfied with the channels already mentioned, send me an email at aquatonkonsults@gmail.com. I'll connect you to the market.

24. I am so interested in fish farming, but the only source of water available to me is rainwater, can I go ahead?

Answer:
Rainwater is good for fish culture. There's nothing wrong with it; only that it must be from clean iron sheets. That is, if you have iron sheets as your roof, you can use the water collected for catfish culture as the pH is safe enough, but if it is asbestos roof, you can't use its trapped water for fishes. It's not that good. But always remember to verify the suitability of your water (regardless of the source) for fish culture before going ahead. It will save you a lot of trouble.

25. The pH of my water was tested to be 4.0, very acidic, how do I neutralize it?

Answer:
All you need to do is to get a liming material, which can be quicklime/slake lime with application at $20 - 50g/m^2$ or agricultural lime at $50 - 200g/m^2$. Also, you can use bicarbonate of soda or soda ash to boost the water until it is normal. There's no stress about that.

26. When do I treat my fish stock? And with what?

Answer:
Treatment in fish is better as prophylactic (preventive) than as therapeutic (curative). You don't have to wait until your fish are sick before you treat. The treatment given to them is mainly to boost their immunity so as to survive any likely attack or infection. Some of the drugs that can be used are: Fish Vit plus, - a multivitamin supplement, Fish biotics - an anitibiotics, Aquaceryl plus – a broad spectrum drug against both gram +ve and gram –ve bacteria among other pathogens, Aquadex, Keproceryl WSP, $KMnO_4$, - Potassium permanganate, MX 1–4, etc. They however have dosages of administration, thus, an expert's prescription would be needed so as not to generate more trouble.
But, as to when, you can treat them once in a month with any of the above mentioned medications (as prescribed by your consultant). And

peradventure there is a disease condition, the same drugs are still applicable, but at different dosages. If you are very faithful in your management practices, you may never experience any disease condition all through your culture period. It's very possible.

27. What are the symptoms of disease to watch out for in my fish?

Answer:
The presence of disease in fish is identified by the following symptoms: loss of appetite; weak, slow or erratic movement; appearance of blood spots on some parts of the body (haemorrhage);presence of wounds on the skin (ulceration and necrosis); frayed or chopped fins and tail; presence of boil-like structures on the body (lesions); appearance of pale, bloody and puffy gills; skin discolouration and patches on the skin; bulging of the eyes; swellings, nodules, sears and blisters; jumping and flashing; loss of weight; poor or stunted growth; bone deformations; mass mortality in pond; gasping at water surface; spiral movement; slaying of scales; loss of balance; crowding at water inlet or outlet etc. All these are symptoms of infection or disease condition, not only in catfish but also in other culturable species, and treatment should not be delayed once any of these is noticed.

28. When can a female broodstock be re-used after breeding?

Answer:
The period between a female broodstock's first use and the second use is called the recycling period. And this period is usually between 3 – 5 months. That is, a female can be re used after about 3 – 5 months after the initial use. But it is noteworthy that during recycling period, good food capable of developing more eggs in it is being given to it (like feeds specially formulated for broodstocks) and the water should also be conducive enough for its survival. They are always weak after the stress of stripping, thus, they should be gently and adequately taken care of (in the spent tank) if they must be reused.

29. Can I put Tilapia and Catfish in the same pond?

Answer:
The answer is yes, and that is what is called polyculture. These species are interdependent on each other especially in terms of food relationship. Tilapia is highly prolific i.e. they reproduce massively thus having the tendency to overpopulate the pond, but with catfish which is carnivorous, they can be fed upon thereby controlling their population. And that is why the stocking ratio is minimum of 3 catfish: 2 tilapia and maximum of 5 catfish: 2 tilapia

30. I have a problem using the sinking feed i.e pelletized feed. I don't know when to stop feeding and I don't see my fish when eating this bothers me, can I be enlightened please?

Answer:
Well, this is not a problem; it's only a challenge that comes with change. But I'll like to inform you right away that catfish are benthic fishes i.e. bottom dwellers by nature. And this means most of their activities, of which feeding is part, takes place at the pond bottom. Coming up to eat floating feed is never their natural way of feeding, it was an artificial configuration adopted by certain farmers. Now, I'm not saying floating feed is bad, only that sinking feed which catfish can take at the pond bottom is better because it better simulates what obtains in their natural habitat. As regards feeding the right quantity, you can sample your fish population to know their average weight so as to determine the quantity they would be fed with. This is because catfish feed with respect to their body weights. You can refer to the answer to question number 7 for more explanation on the sampling issue. Concerning seeing your fish, you can see them if you ensure your water is not turbid or dirty. But before you introduce the sinking feed if you've been giving them floating feed before, skip some regimes or starve them for almost a full day so that they can receive the new feed. This is normal because they have been used to a type before thus to change the feed, there must be a gap or else they would not take it.

31. Somebody said I have to fertilize my concrete tank with fowl droppings or cow dung before stocking. Is it good?

Answer:
It would have been good if it were to be an earthen pond. The essence of fertilization is to make the pond water productive through the presence of algae (phytoplanktons). These phytoplanktons need sunlight to photosynthesize and the moment they emerge, the zooplanktons that feed on them are made available. These zooplanktons which feed on the phytoplanktons are in turn eaten by the catfish. If you fertilize the concrete tank, the algae will come up, but I bet you, you'll soon have problems reducing them. This is because, algae occurs in the concrete tanks exposed to sunlight without fertilization, and even then, we still find ways of controlling it as too much of it prevents the availability of dissolved oxygen to the fish, capable of triggering mortality. Don't bother fertilizing your concrete tank; just rinse/wash after construction, impound with water and stock. The fish will be fine.

32. When is the best time to transport my fish? And with what?

Answer:
The best times to transport fish are before the sun comes out and after the sun must have gone down i.e early in the morning and late in the evening. The reason is that fishes, being aquatic animals are poikilothermic (cold blooded) and as a result get stressed when exposed to sunlight; especially when not in their natural habitat. Transportation will involve taking the fish out of water into a container, and this if done when the sun is up can trigger mortality due to stress. Also, medium and method of transportation are of importance here. There are various containers that can be used to transport fish. These include oxygenated bags, foldable fibre bags, jerry cans, plastic containers etc. Any of these can be used to convey fish from one place to another. But care must be taken to ensure they are not packed in such a way that they will be choked up. They should be spread, and with clean water which can be changed along the road if the journey is a little bit far. Also, the fish should have more space to itself, when travelling a long distance, this will minimize the stress.

33. How do I introduce by newly bought fish into the pond?

Answer:
The moment you arrive with your fish, lower the container into the already impounded pond i.e pond with water already pumped in. Let the water in the pond mix with the water in your container and the moment the fishes feel comfortable with the new water (which has mixed with the one they were brought in) they will swim out on their own into the new water, and they will be able to acclimatize. This is very important, as pouring the fish into the strange water may lead to temperature shock, and ultimately resulting in mortality. They are to be left for about 3 – 4 hours to get used to the new medium, after which feed can be given to them. If they refuse the feed; it's no problem, they are only trying to adapt to the new environment, and as soon as they do that, they will start feeding. In addition to this, certain drugs like aquaceryl, formalin etc serve as anti-stress to the fish and as such can be applied on prescription.

34. What is this cannibalism? And how can I handle it?

Answer:
Cannibalism is a condition whereby animals (carnivorous or omnivorous) prey on other living animals. That is, cannibalism occurs when an animal eats another animal alive for whatever reason. In catfish however, this cannot be totally ruled out as it is part of their genetic make-up. There are two types of cannibalism in fish culture; type A – when a fish totally swallows another fish from the head to tail without any remainder of the fish and type B – when a fish swallows another fish from the tail but leaves the skull (head) in the water uneaten. Cannibalism can as well be due to inadequate feeding, overpopulation, stocking of different fish sizes together etc. Thus, to remedy it, sort and grade your fish stock regularly (every 2 – 3 weeks) until you have averagely uniform sizes stocked in the ponds. Also, feed adequately and stock at correct stocking densities.

35. What is the optimum temperature required for Clarias culture?

Answer:
The temperature is in a range. And the best range for clarias culture is between 27°C – 30°C. At this temperature, they will thrive well and carryout all their activities in the water comfortably. A thermometer can be used to measure this.

36. I bought some fingerlings, but they refused to grow, can you explain this?

Answer:
Yes, I can. You see, whenever you decide to purchase fingerlings, check the history of the place of purchase. Who has bought from them before? How has their product been doing in previous times? Are there complaints of any sort about the farm or the person selling them to you? These are parts of the questions to ask. This is because some people sell runts to customers in the name of fingerlings. Runts are fishes that are genetically impaired as far as their growth is concerned. They don't grow like others, no matter how you feed them. They are genetically like that. So, what some people do is that they sort them out and sell them to buyers in the name of fingerlings, which is against the ethics of the profession. If you are so unfortunate to be a recipient of such wicked act, you may feed them heaven and earth, they will not grow; and it's not their fault, they just can't grow. On the other hand, if you bought good fingerlings and suddenly they stopped growing, check your water pH and the feed you are giving them. Is your pH at the optimum range conducive for fish culture? And is your feed made up of the right ingredients in their right proportions? Check these and make necessary corrections where needed, and you'll overcome the problem.

37. There was a time I wanted to breed, but the female broodstock died after injection, why?

Answer:

This could be traced to many things. It could be that the female had been stressed up before the injection probably having travelled a long distance to the point of use, or has been subjected to a lot of stress in the process of bringing it out of the water. Also, if two or more females are kept together in a single container prior injection, they must have fought and probably injured themselves, causing great stress.

Another thing is that if an overdose of hormone is injected into the fish, it may not react well to it. And if the point of injection is not the right place (i.e the dorsal muscle), it could trigger off any adverse condition. In addition to this, an infected fish or a disease carrier may die when taken out of the water, especially if the pathogen has incubated long enough in the fish and has actually completed its life cycle in the fish up to a lethal stage. The fish in this case is already gone, and injecting such fish with hormone may accelerate its mortality. Furthermore, haemorrhage i.e internal bleeding may lead to death in an injected female.

38. What is the relationship between good water quality and fish growth?

Answer:

Fishes are aquatic organisms and as result will not survive elsewhere than in the water. All the characteristics of living things as far as fishes are concerned take place in their habitat, which is water. These characteristics include nutrition, growth, movement, reproduction, respiration, excretion etc, and for fish, they all take place in the water. However, for fish to grow, certain parameters would have to be in place. For instance, feeding is what leads to growth and feeding would not take place if certain parameters in the water are inadequate or absent. For fishes to eat and behave well, the pH of the water will have to be the right one, the temperature will have to be conducive, the ammonia content will have to be kept at the conducive range, the dissolved oxygen and transparency will have to be at the right amount etc. These, when optimum or simply put, when good, give fishes a good environment to grow and develop, carrying out other activities of living things. It is as well important to note that without good respiration (as made available by dissolved oxygen, which is one of the parameters that make up the water quality, the fish will not even stay alive let alone growing. Therefore, the relationship between good water quality and fish growth is that the latter will not be possible without the former i.e. fish growth depends on how good the quality of the water is, knowing that they can't survive or grow elsewhere.

39. I want my fish to grow big within a short time, can I get a growth enhancer?

Answer:
The use of growth hormone is prohibited. It's against the ethics of aquaculture practice. This is because the growth hormones when used to raise fish to a certain size before its normal time of reaching such size form certain deposits in the fish tissues – making the fish a very dangerous fish to eat. The fishes when eaten by human have the tendency to trigger hyper secretion of certain body hormones leading to malfunctioning of the glands secreting such hormones. For instance, in a developing child, the effect can be one hand growing bigger than the other, or a part of the brain growing bigger than the other. It affects the genetic and hormonal make-up of the consumers, and as a result; it's a criminal practice.

If you want your fish to grow, buy good fish seeds, give them good and high quality feed (with all the ingredients in right proportion) and ensure they have good space (i.e stocking at right densities), they will surely grow. Remember that any of your family members may fall victim of the detrimental effects of these growth hormones when your fish finally gets to the market. What goes round comes round.

40. I am a fish farmer, but I didn't study Agriculture in school, am I in any way disadvantaged?

Answer:
The answer can be yes or no. There are two types of education, the formal and the informal education. The formal speaks of what you go to school to study while the informal talks of what you learn outside

school. And in the world of entrepreneurs, informal education plays a greater role in their success than the formal education. So, if you sit down and accept your doom of not studying agriculture in school, the answer is yes, you are disadvantaged. But if you can climb a sycamore tree like Zacchaeus in the Bible, your short stature will not prevent you from seeing Jesus. That is, if you can launch out and acquire the skills involved in the practice informally – which can be by reading books on it, browsing the internet or better still acquiring training from a well-established fish farm; the answer will be no, you are not disadvantaged. The choice is however yours to make.

41. I am a fish farmer, but I need a good consultant for good results, can you recommend any?

Answer:
Yes, the author of this book is one and you can contact him through email at aquatonkonsults@yahoo.com. He will tell you the modalities involved when you contact him. Your decision to get a consultant is a good one. It helps a lot.

42. I have discovered over time that people sell runts as fingerlings, can you recommend any farm that I can patronize where such won't be done?

Answer:
I have many farms with integrity as their watchwords. But to prevent unauthorized advertisement. Email me confidentially, and I will link you up.

43. How do I preserve my ovaprim hormone after use?

Answer:
You are to keep it in a cool, dry place. And this can be in your table drawer, on a safe shelf, in your wardrobe, or even inside your refrigerator (not deep freezer). It's just to keep it fresh. Ensure it is covered and properly kept. Also keep out of the reach of children and others who don't

know its use so as not to create an avenue for poisoning. It's for fish, not for home use.

44. If I have more milt left after breeding, how do I preserve it, and for how long?

Answer:
As scarce as good milt can be, it's unfortunate that it cannot stay for long once squeezed out. If you are faced with this condition, you can keep the remaining in the refrigerator (not freezer) for about 12 –24 hours after which it may coagulate and become useless. The cells are very sensitive to environmental changes and may not actually yield good results after a long time. Try as much as possible not to have left over.

45. When fishes start dying, what is the first thing to do?

Answer:
The first thing to do is to stop feeding, and drain off the water. After putting in fresh water, you can begin to query the condition, using the symptoms noticed as indicators in tracking down the cause of the situation, before knowing the treatment to give. You have to stop feeding because it's most likely more of the served feed would be uneaten thus making the water more unconducive for them through ammonia generation.

46. How can I reduce the risk of infection in my pond?

Answer:
You can do this by faithfully following all the management practices involved in fish farming. For instance, you must scrutinize the source of your fish seeds (fingerlings/juveniles) to be sure they are not carriers of infection. You are to feed fresh (not expired or fermented) feeds, you are to change your water as and when due. You are to prevent indiscriminate introduction of any unclean material or implement into the water, you are to rinse your plastics among other things you make use of with salt from time to time. You are to sanitize the pond environ-

ment, you are not to introduce any foreign/wild fish into your stock without quarantining. You are to take note of any deviation of the fishes from their normal behaviour early enough and administer prophylactic (preventive) treatments, you are to ensure they are not stressed because the moment they are stressed, their immunity become low and they become vulnerable to any infection. To minimize stress, they are to be fed regularly, they are not to be worked upon under direct sunlight i.e you should not carry out any operation on them (like sorting, counting, grading etc) under the sun. You are also not to keep them out of water for too long. If all these are faithfully practiced, you are very much likely to have an infection free culture or at least, a reduced likelihood of infection.

47. Can fishes raised in earthen ponds survive in concrete tanks?

Answer:
Yes, they can, only that it is not the best. This is because fishes raised in earthen ponds have access to certain natural foods, mainly zooplanktons like moina, daphnia and other Cladocerans. They feed on these microorganisms at will, making them to be less dependent on the supplied feed. But when you bring such fish from their comfort region to a region where you will have to feed them or nothing happens, they find it difficult to adapt and most times they don't thrive well until after a long time when of course they would have been forced to adapt. On the other hand, taking concrete tank raised fishes to the earthen pond is like sending them from Egypt to Canaan land. They would be so happy there, because earthen pond simulates their natural habitats more than the concrete tanks. That's the reason they are called mud fishes i.e catfish. They are benthic and they dwell more in the muddy areas of the pond. Concrete tanks do not have muds. Note however that this explanation is not intended to cancel concrete tank practice, it is just to answer the question asked. There is no one way to fish farming, there are many ways.

48. Can I use tap water for fish culture?

Answer:
Yes, you can use it, but you will have to age it first. Tap water is chlorinated and must be aged for 24 hours before use to allow the chlorine gas to evaporate. To age means to expose the water to the atmosphere for evaporation to occur. This is very necessary as chlorine is poisonous to fish. After 24 hours, the water can be used to culture fish.

49. I'm just doing this fish farming business and I keep spending money. I don't even know if I'm making profit or not. How can I correct this?

Answer:
May I first and foremost congratulate you for asking this question. The first step in proffering solution to any problem is to first identify the problem. Doing any business without a feasibility study is gambling. To venture into any project involving capital, you must take your time to survey and get facts about the business. It is these facts that will assist your choices and influence your decision making process. The facts derived will tell you what to expect in the business and will properly guide you in making reasonable projections.

On commencement of the business however, there should be records of all kinds, relating all that is going on in the business. Such records include the credit and debit account, the profit and loss account, purchases, income and expenditure analysis, loans record etc. These records will let you know how you are performing in business. If you just keep spending money without knowing if you are making profit or not, you can be sure you'll soon be out of business. To correct the problem you've identified, get books and start recording your purchases, incomes, granted loans, credit sales, mortality, quantity of feed given weekly, or monthly, stocking dates, harvest dates, etc. Make sure you record everything you spend money on no matter how trivial it appears to be and all the money received should be documented as well. Review them from time to time. And having batched your stocks, take an overall account at the end of each batch's sale; this will tell you what you realized from the batch or the loss you incurred from it, it's either way.

If you don't have time for all these details, employ someone in the accounting field to do it for you. It worths it if you must remain in business.

50. How can I prevent flooding in my tank, especially whenever rain falls heavily?

Answer:

In the construction of concrete tanks; there is what we call overflow channel or overflow pipe. It is an opening located at the side of the pond at a height the farmer doesn't want water to exceed. For instance, for a tank of 1.5m depth, the farmer may put the overflow pipe at 1.2m height. This means, any time water attempts to rise above this 1.2m level, it will start draining out through the pipe. In this way, there will never be a time that the water will be above 1.2m either rain falls or not. This is the way to prevent flood from carrying the fishes away during heavy down pours. If your pond does not have it, try and put it. You can contact your plumber. But if you desire to raise the water above that marked level, especially during dry season, all you need to do is to cork it i.e. you close it and water will rise beyond it.

Please, remember this; whenever this overflow pipe is operational i.e. whenever it is in use, ensure the inner one (inside the tank) is screened with a net so that some fish will not go out with the water.

CONCLUSION

The answers provided to the asked questions are facts acquired through years of experience as a fisheries expert and consultant. You are therefore encouraged to apply them as they suit your own case.

For any form of enquiries,
Email: aquatonkonsults@yahoo.com

ABOUT THE AUTHOR

Prince Anthony Adefarakan as he is popularly called is the M.D/CEO of Aquaton Konsults, Nigeria, West Africa. He is an experienced Fisheries Consultant with vast wealth of knowledge in matters relating to fish production. He has practically demonstrated artificial fish breeding, fish ponds construction, fish feeding, fish disease and management among other fish production techniques to a large number of farmers far and wide. In addition to training these farmers (some of which are students, retirees and investors), he has been personally involved in their business set up; providing the necessary resources to ensure their success.

At some point in his Fisheries career, he served as a Master Aquaculture Service Provider (MASP) to a Department for International Development (DFID) funded project in the Niger Delta part of Nigeria (Market Development Project in the Niger Delta). He also served as one of the USAID's Nigerian Agricultural Enterprise Curriculum (NAEC) trainers in the Niger Delta.

His impact was felt in academics as well. He was a lecturer and also the personnel appointed to handle the Fisheries section of the World Bank funded STEP-B Project of the Federal College of Education (Technical), Asaba where he had the opportunity to impact the Agriculture students of the institution with relevant aquaculture knowledge capable of making them self-reliant upon graduation. Furthermore, he has had the opportunity to serve as one of the

Fisheries Examiners and Moderators for West African Examination Council.

This book is therefore a compressed presentation of both his theoretical and field expertise. For successful fish production at all levels, this handbook is a must read

He currently lives in Canada with his family.

www.ingramcontent.com/pod-product-compliance
Lightning Source LLC
Chambersburg PA
CBHW070037040426
42333CB00040B/1708